I0811821

Spotlight on Colorado

THE FIRST COLORADANS

Native Americans in Colorado

Ruth Lohr

PowerKiDS press

NEW YORK

Published in 2016 by The Rosen Publishing Group, Inc.
29 East 21st Street, New York, NY 10010

Copyright © 2016 by The Rosen Publishing Group, Inc.

All rights reserved. No part of this book may be reproduced in any form without permission in writing from the publisher, except by a reviewer.

Editor: Debbie Nevins
Book Design: Iron Cupcake Design

Cataloging-in-Publication Data

Lohr, Ruth.
The first Coloradans: Native Americans in Colorado / by Ruth Lohr.
p. cm. — (Spotlight on Colorado)
Includes index.
ISBN 978-1-4994-1444-8 (pbk.)
ISBN 978-1-4994-1446-2 (6 pack)
ISBN 978-1-4994-1448-6 (library binding)
1. Indians of North America — Colorado — Juvenile literature. 2. Colorado — History — Juvenile literature. I. Title.
E78.C6 L64 2016
978.8'00497—d23

Photo Credits: Videowokart/Shutterstock.com, cover; Jim Lambert/Shutterstock.com, 3; Planet Observer/UIG/ Universal Images Group/Getty Images, 5; Roblespepe/File:Peopling of America through Beringia.png/Wikimedia Commons, 6; Heinrich Harder (1858-1935)/File:Glyptodon old drawing.jpg/Wikimedia Commons, 7; Nicolas Primola/Shutterstock.com, 7; Virginia Dept. of Historic Resources./File:Clovis Point.jpg/Wikimedia Commons, 8; Peter V. Bianchi/National Geographic/Getty Images, 9; Sethant/File:Soapstone-LindenmeierSite.JPG/Wikimedia Commons, 10; Kenneth Murray/Getty Images, 12; Dorling Kindersley/Getty Images, 13; Jeffrey M. Frank/Shutterstock.com, 13; Marc Venema/Shutterstock.com, 14; Cardaf/Shutterstock.com, 15; sydcinema/Shutterstock.com, 15; Bob Palin/File:Crnp moki cliff 041031.jpg/Wikimedia Commons, 16; Brian Lee/File:PillingFigurines01.jpg/Wikimedia Commons, 17; Smithsonian American Art Museum/File:BuffaloHunters.jpg/Wikimedia Commons, 18; aragami1/Shutterstock.com, 19; Denver Public Library/File:IndianTravois.jpg/Wikimedia Commons, 19; SuperStock/ Getty Images, 20; altrendo travel/Getty Images, 21; Rose and Hopkins, Denver, Colorado/ LCUSZ62111566/Library of Congress, 23; Balster, Frank S/cph 3c12572/Library of Congress, 24; Chris Light/File:003 Knife River Village Buffalo Robe.jpg/Wikimedia Commons, 26; MPI/ Getty Images, 27; Edward S. Curtis/File:Apache Wickiup, Edward Curtis, 1903.jpg/Wikimedia Commons, 28; Rose, Noah H./File:Apache wickiup.jpg/Wikimedia Commons, 29; Unknown/ File:UteHideArt3.jpg/Wikimedia Commons, 29; LCUSZ62111572/Library of Congress. 30; Henry Johnson/cph 3c11572/Library of Congress, 31; William Perry/iStock/Thinkstock, 31; © AP Photo, 32; MPI/Getty Images, 33; De Agostini Picture Library/Getty Images, 35; MPI/Getty Images, 36; Mathew Brady/File:Ute delegation.jpg/Wikimedia Commons, 37; Fraser, Clayton/BHABS CO-176-A/Library of Congress, 38; Census.gov/File:Americanindiansmapcensusbureau.gif/ Wikimedia Commons, 39; unknown/File:Teacher with picture cards giving English instruction to Navajo day school students - NARA - 295158.tif/Wikimedia Commons, 40; Phaedriel/File:Carlisle pupils.jpg/Wikimedia Commons, 41; David W. Hamilton/Getty Images, 43; Ss114/File: Housing Characteristics on Reservations.png/Wikimedia Commons, 44; AP Photo/David Zalubowski, 45.

Manufactured in the United States of America

CPSIA Compliance Information: Batch #BS15PK: For further information contact Rosen Publishing, New York, New York at 1-800-237-9932

Contents

Some of the tribes that lived and hunted in parts of Colorado include the:

Apache
Arapaho
Cheyenne
Comanche
Jicarilla
Kiowa
Navajo
Pueblo
Shoshone
Ute

CHAPTER 1

Tribes and Nations

People lived on this land long before it was called Colorado. We call them the first Coloradans, but the people had other names for the land and for themselves. They called themselves *Hinono-eino* or *Inuna-ina*, meaning "the people." They had many languages and many names. They were the Ute [YOOT], the Arapaho [uh-RAA-puh-hoh], the Cheyenne [shy-AN], and others. These are the names of their **tribes**, or nations.

The map shows where the tribes lived. But lines on a map can't really tell us this information. Many tribes moved from place to place within a large region. They often shared their land with other tribes, and sometimes their territories overlapped. Native people didn't think in terms of owning the land, though they did occasionally fight with other tribes for access to certain terrain.

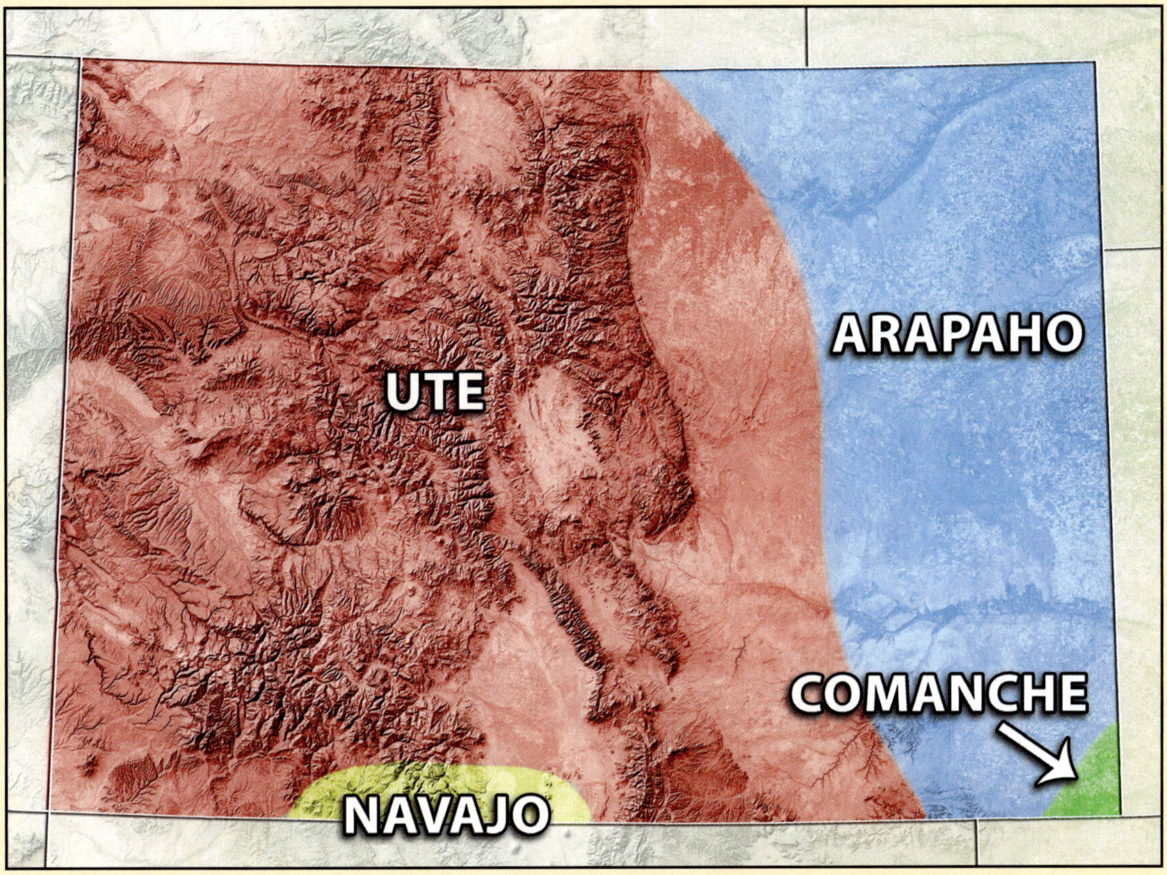

This map of Colorado shows approximately where the tribes lived. The rough regions are the mountains.

The native people did not draw maps, so no written records exist of the times before the Europeans came. It's best to think of the lines on this map as approximate and always in motion, drifting this way and that over time.

Of course, once the white settlers arrived, everything changed.

FIRST PEOPLE

The first people to occupy a certain territory—anywhere in the world—are called native, indigenous, or aboriginal people.

A
BRIDGE TO
SOMEWHERE

The prehistoric land bridge from Asia to North America is called Beringia.

CHAPTER 2

Paleo-Indians

Who were the very first people to live in Colorado? Where did they come from?

Archaeologists study human history by digging up bones, tools, and other things early

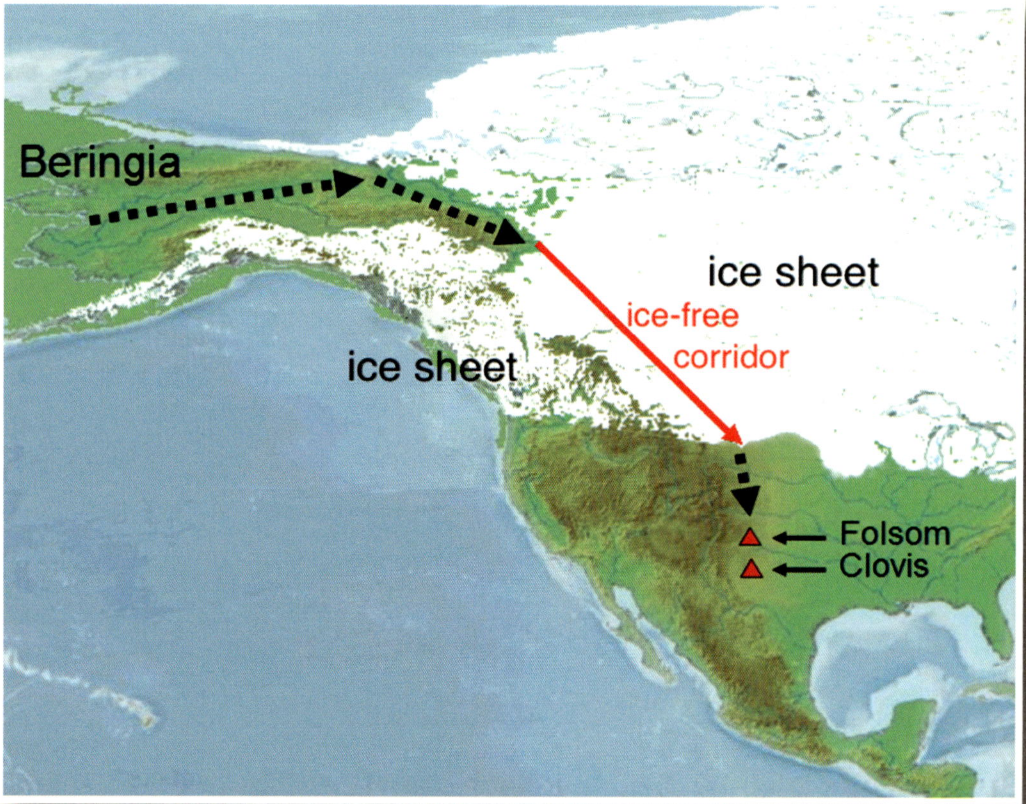

The earliest people probably came to North America across a land bridge that connected regions of today's Russia and Alaska.

This illustration pictures how early native people might have hunted an animal called a glyptodon, now extinct.

people left behind. They believe humans first came to North America from Asia around 30,000 to 15,000 years ago. Tribes slowly migrated across the Bering Sea on a narrow strip of land and ice. That land connection between Russia and Alaska no longer exists; the rising ocean covered it long ago.

We call those people the Paleo-Indians. When they first came to Colorado, the land and climate were in a period of great change.

BIG BEASTS

Mammoths were distant relatives of the mastodon and far more widespread. Various species lived in Africa, Europe, and Asia as well as North America.

FEET OF STONE

The oldest known human footprints in North America are 10,550 years old. They were discovered in 1961 in Mexico, 186 miles (300 km) south of Texas. The ancient traveler's prints in the mineral-rich desert soil hardened into stone over time.

Mastodons became extinct around 10,000 years ago. They were similar in appearance to elephants and lived only in North America.

An **ice age** was ending. Melting **glaciers** revealed the Rocky Mountains. Receding ice carved out the mesas. Large mammals roamed the land—mastodon, mammoth, giant sloth, camel, and the ancient bison. They're all now extinct.

Here, the people found plentiful food. In addition to large and small mammals, they found abundant fish and birds in the rivers, lakes, and marshes. They gathered nuts, berries, and edible plants. Family groups of about 20 to 60 people roamed the Great Plains, following the animals, never staying in one place very long.

Primitive Tools

Near Littleton, Colorado, archaeologists found rough tools made of flint buried among the bones of ancient mammals. The people used these sharpened stones for hunting, as well as for cutting and scraping animal hides. They ate the meat and used the hides for clothing and shelter.

American Indians probably began using bows and arrows around 1,500 years ago.

CHAPTER 3

Ancient Cultures

Over several thousand years, different cultures of Paleo-Indians lived in this region. Archaeologists sort the cultures according to the **artifacts**, or things the people made. Distinct types of tools, spear points, and projectiles tell us how and where the people lived. Animal bones bearing carving marks tell us what they ate.

Artifacts from the Folsom culture were found at the Lindenmeier Site in the Soapstone Prairie Natural Area near Fort Collins, Colorado.

The Canyons of the Ancients National Monument in southwestern Colorado was created in 2000 to protect Ancestral Puebloan ruins. However, the park has suffered from severe episodes of looting and vandalism. Thousands of artifacts have been stolen.

Archaeologists have identified more than 56,500 sites of prehistoric humans in Colorado. They date from about 12,000 BC to the 19th century.

During this period, the climate warmed. The land became drier, and food was not as abundant. The larger mammals died out, and the Paleo people had to adapt. They depended more on bison and smaller mammals and gathered wild plants to supplement their diets.

Toward the end of this period, the people learned to grow and store their food.

Paleo-Indian Cultures	When	Characteristics	Colorado Archaeological Sites
Clovis	13,000 to 12,000 years ago	Possibly the ancestors of most of the various native peoples in the Americas. Hunted large ice-age mammals.	Dent Site near Milliken, Mahaffy Cache in Boulder
Folsom complex	11,000 to 10,000 years ago	As ice-age mammals died out, this culture hunted bison and smaller mammals. Lived in small, multifamily groups.	Lindenmeier Site near Fort Collins
Plano cultures (includes Cody complex and others)	10,000 to 7,000 years ago	Hunted bison by forcing stampedes off cliffs or into corrals.	Olsen-Chubbuck Bison Kill Site near Kit Carson
Archaic	7,000 to 1,500 years ago	Made baskets and pottery to store food; cultivated maize (corn); built shelters with wood	Magic Mountain Site near Golden

KNOWLEDGE NUGGET

Some researchers think the large ice-age mammals that once lived in North America became extinct because of overhunting by the Clovis people. Climate change also altered the animals' habitats and could have led to extinction.

CHAPTER 4

The Mystery of the Cliff Dwellers

Once you have planted seed in the ground, you need to care for your crop and harvest its fruit. In other words, you have to stay in one place. Staying in one place means you can build more permanent shelters. These changes affected the lifestyles of the early Indian cultures.

Rock carvings called petroglyphs decorate the walls of the Ancestral Puebloan cliff dwellings of Mesa Verde.

Most of the Four Corners region belongs to several Native American tribes that have reservations there.

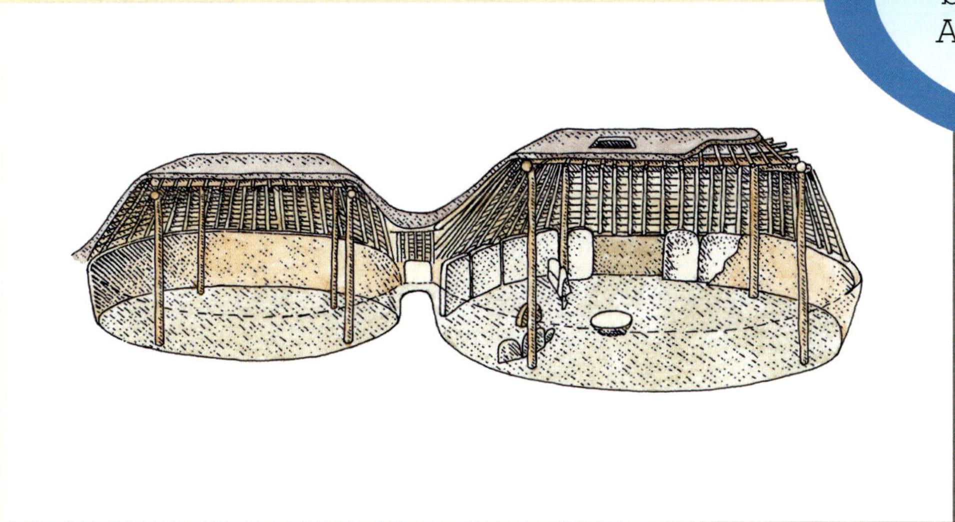

This diagram shows the structure of a typical pit house.

In Colorado's southwestern Four Corners region, a new culture arose around 1,400 years ago. The people built houses on mesa tops. Today we call those people the Ancestral Puebloans. *Pueblo* is a Spanish word meaning "village." The people lived in "pit houses" made of wood and mud built over a shallow hole dug into the earth.

WHERE YOU CAN BE IN FOUR STATES AT ONCE

The Four Corners is the point where the southwest corner of Colorado meets New Mexico, Arizona, and Utah. This plaque, left, marks the spot. It's the only location in the US where four states meet.

Groups of tourists admire the ancient sandstone dwellings in Mesa Verde National Park.

But then, after living on the mesa tops for about 600 years, the people suddenly moved down into the cliffsides. They built small cities of brick into, and under, the overhanging cliffs of Mesa Verde. These mysterious sandstone buildings look like castles with rooms, passageways, tunnels, and steps. The occupants decorated the walls with earthen plasters of pink, brown, red, yellow, and white. Some of the biggest dwellings have more than 100 rooms!

THE ANCIENT ANCESTORS

The Ancestral Puebloans are sometimes referred to as the Anasazi people. The name comes from a Navajo word meaning "ancient ones" or "ancient enemy." However, today's Pueblo people prefer the term Ancestral Puebloans.

Mesa Verde National Park protects some 4,700 archaeological sites, including 600 cliff dwellings.

The remarkable structures are among the best preserved cliff dwellings in North America.

The Ancestral Puebloans lived in the cliff dwellings for only about 100 years. Then, around the year AD 1300, they disappeared. No one knows why they left.

KNOWLEDGE NUGGET

Colorado's Mesa Verde National Park was established in 1906 by President Theodore Roosevelt. It was the first national park of its kind.

ROCK ARTISTS

The canyons of Dinosaur National Monument, a park on the border of Colorado and Utah, reveal the presence of the Freemont people some 800 to 1,200 years ago. They left behind petroglyphs and pictographs (rock carvings and paintings) that can still be seen today.

CHAPTER 5

People of the Colorado Plateau

Fremont People, AD 700 1300

Around the same time that the Ancestral Pueblo culture was thriving, another native culture was living in Colorado. The Fremont people lived farther north, on the Western Slope. Like the Puebloans, the Fremont built pit houses in villages of 10 to up to 100 homes. They also lived in **wickiups** (brush and log huts) and natural rock shelters, such as caves.

The Fremont people stored grain in the crevice of this cliff.

The Fremont people were hunters and gatherers, but they also farmed. They grew corn, squash, and beans. They

These clay figurines are some of the artifacts left behind by the Fremont culture of Native Americans.

ground the corn into meal between two flat stone surfaces. The cornmeal was then stored in pottery jars inside brick buildings called granaries.

Perhaps the most fascinating artifacts the Fremont left behind were clay figurines. The small figures resemble people, with tiny details such as ear bobs, necklaces, clothing, hair, and facial decorations. Were these little figures dolls or puppets? No one knows, but experts believe they were probably used for religious or magical purposes.

Around AD 1300 or so, the Fremont culture vanished. Just as with the Ancestral Puebloans, no one is quite sure why.

WHERE DID THEY GO?
Historians think the Fremont people might have died out due to drought or other change of environment. Alternatively, they might have been conquered or absorbed by other Indian cultures.

MYSTERIOUS FORMS

Fremont rock art portrays simplified, geometric human forms. It also shows animals, such as bighorn sheep, birds, snakes, and lizards, as well as abstract and geometrical designs, including circles and spirals. Their meaning or purpose is unknown.

CHAPTER 6

Buffalo Hunters of the Great Plains

By the time American explorers and fur traders came to Colorado's eastern plains in the early 1800s, it was home to the Plains Indians. These were the buffalo hunters. The largest tribes

Before the Plains Indians had horses, they used surprising methods to hunt bison. In this painting from 1833, they sneak up close to the herd disguised as wolves.

The ancestors of the Arapaho came to the Great Plains from the western Great Lakes region sometime before 1700.

TEEPEE

were the Cheyenne and the Arapaho in the Northern and Central Plains. South of the Arkansas River were the Comanche.

These were **nomadic** people, meaning they moved around. They followed the great herds of buffalo, or bison, that roamed the plains. The people used the animals for more than just meat. The Plains Indians lived in **teepees** made from buffalo skins. Such structures suited the nomadic lifestyle because they could be easily raised and easily taken down.

NO WHEELS

When teepees were taken apart, their poles were made into a drag sled called a travois (truh-VOY). Two teepee poles formed the framework, and a platform was suspended between them. Belongings—and even children—could be packed onto that platform. The sled was pulled by horses or dogs.

KNOWLEDGE NUGGET

WORKING DOGS
Before the Arapaho acquired horses, they used domestic dogs as pack animals to pull loads.

The Horse

The horse was originally native to North America. However, along with other large mammals, the species went extinct on this continent about 12,000 years ago. Long before dying out here, though, the species migrated to other continents, where it survived.

When Spanish explorers arrived in the early 1500s, they brought horses. Over time, some animals escaped and formed herds of wild horses, called mustangs. It didn't take long for the native people to make them their own.

Skilled horsemen could hunt bison from horseback using bows and arrows.

A bronze statue of an Indian warrior on horseback stands in the Civic Center Park in downtown Denver.

Horses changed the Indians' way of life forever. Horses enabled hunters to pursue bison at great speeds. Horses also allowed the people to travel greater distances for trade. The animals helped transport the tribe's belongings. This meant the people could acquire more and heavier possessions, and they did.

Horses carried weak, old, and sick tribal members, who might earlier have been abandoned. Not least, horses brought about a new form of warfare between tribes—and eventually against the Americans.

TWO-WAY TRAFFIC

Horses probably migrated from North America to Asia the same way people came from Asia to North America—across the prehistoric land bridge between the two continents.

CHAPTER 7

The People of the West

The Ute (YOOT) people once lived across almost all of Colorado. Their hunting grounds extended even farther. According to tribal history, the people have been here since the beginning of time. That story has been handed down from generation to generation over many centuries.

Scientifically, that may not be quite accurate. But the Ute are probably the people who have been here the longest. They lived in the mountains and vast areas of Colorado, Utah, Wyoming, eastern Nevada, northern New Mexico, and Arizona.

Within this huge tribe were smaller units called bands. The Mouache band, for example, lived on the eastern slopes of the Rockies. The Caputa band lived in the San Luis Valley, near the headwaters of the Rio Grande. Other bands lived on the Western Slope.

One of the states is named for the Ute Indians. Can you figure out which one it is?

Five Ute women pose for a photograph in 1899.

The town of Ignacio, Colorado, was named for the Chief Ignacio. He was the leader of the Southern Utes in the 19th century. Today the town has about 700 people.

Chief Ignacio, pictured here in 1904, was a leader of the Southern Ute tribe.

In the mountain forests of western Colorado, archaeologists have found the remains of at least 366 wickiups. The wooden structures were built by the Ute people more than a century ago.

Like the other native people, the Ute people lived in harmony with their environment. They hunted buffalo, elk, deer, and antelope. They ate berries and roots, and used plants such as the yucca to make soap, rope, shoes, mats, and baskets. The people had deep knowledge of the medicinal power of plants. As they traveled throughout their lands, the Ute established trails that crisscrossed the mountain ranges. The Ute were one of the first tribes to have horses and quickly became great horsemen.

WRANGLE UP SOME FACTS

ORIGIN STORIES

Almost every culture has a mythological story, such as the Utes', that explains how people came to live on Earth. Such a tale is called an origin story and is one that has been passed on through countless generations. Often the stories include magical creatures such as gods and talking animals or objects, such as the moon and sun. The stories were sacred and believed as truth, though today most are appreciated as cultural myths.

CHAPTER 8

Native Lives: Food, Clothing, Shelter

TALKING TREES

Native peoples did not have written language. However, they used pictures to relay information. Sometimes they carved symbols or images onto tree trunks, usually aspens. Such trees are called message trees.

Indians also bent trees to mark trails or show direction. These are called marker trees. They functioned like early road maps. Researchers have documented 1,850 marker trees in 39 states. Marker trees that are still alive today are at least 150 to 200 years old.

The native people depended on nature for all their needs. They hunted animals for meat and gathered roots, seeds, and berries. Animal hides were made into warm clothing.

The Plains Indians depended greatly on bison. Fresh and dried bison meat made up a large part of their diet. Bison hides served as clothing and floor coverings in their shelters.

An elaborately decorated buffalo robe of the Plains Indians hangs on display.

A family of Plains Indians transports their possessions on a travois, a framework of wooden poles and bison rawhide.

Since the Indians moved frequently, they needed easily portable shelters. Teepees were the perfect answer. The cone-shaped tents were made of poles covered with animal hides. The top was left open so smoke from indoor campfires could escape. In the Plains Indian cultures, the women owned the teepees. Women made them, erected them, and cared for them inside and out. Men never helped with the teepees; it was not their job.

TASTY TREES

The inner bark of aspen trees tastes sweet, and the Utes considered it a delicacy. It could be eaten raw, baked into cakes, or boiled into a syrup. It was given to children as a sweet treat.

BRUSH WICKIUP

The Ute Indians of the West hunted bison as well. Every year, they would travel to the eastern plains to hunt. Back home, they hunted other animals, including deer, elk, and bear. The Ute built shelters called wickiups. These circular domed buildings were made of poles and brush. The poles were young pine,

KNOWLEDGE NUGGET

HEALING TREES

The bark of many kinds of trees, particularly juniper and aspen, was used to make a variety of medicines. Aspen bark, for example, contains salicin, a pain-relieving substance similar to the one found in aspirin.

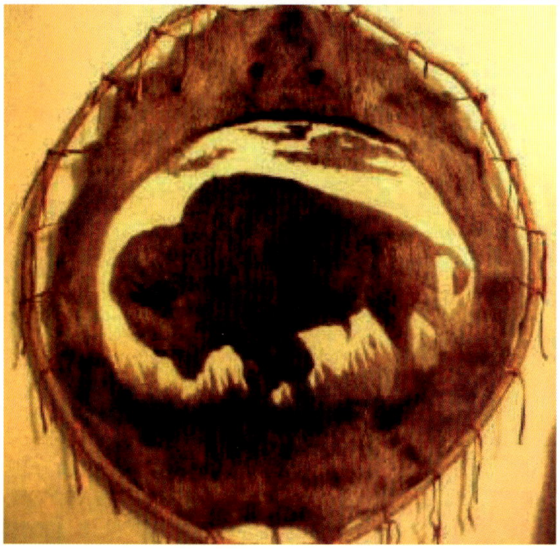

This Ute beaver-hide decoration of a bison dates to the 1800s.

juniper, willow, or aspen trees and branches. Brush was stuffed between the poles. Animal hides might sometimes be used as well.

Native women often carried babies in a type of child carrier called a cradleboard. On a cradleboard, an infant was tightly wrapped in blankets and strapped to a plank of wood or basket fiber with leather or cloth.

CHAPTER 9

Society, Arts, and Culture

Indian life centered on the family and the community. Large, extended families lived close together, connected by the bonds of kinship. Smaller communities were called bands, and each band belonged to a larger tribal community.

An Ute woman holds her baby in a photo from 1899.

Everyone had a job to do. Women gathered and prepared food, made clothing, erected and moved the teepees, and cared for young children. Men tended the horses, made weapons, and hunted. Older children had chores as well. Boys might watch the horses or hunt small animals;

girls would gather food and help their mothers. Elderly relatives also helped with child care.

Once a year, bands came together for a big tribal gathering. These great occasions included religious ceremonies, dances, music, feasts, and the sharing of news and gossip. Musicians played flutes (right), drums, and rattles, and chanted or sang.

For the Plains Indians, the yearly gathering would often include large-scale bison hunts.

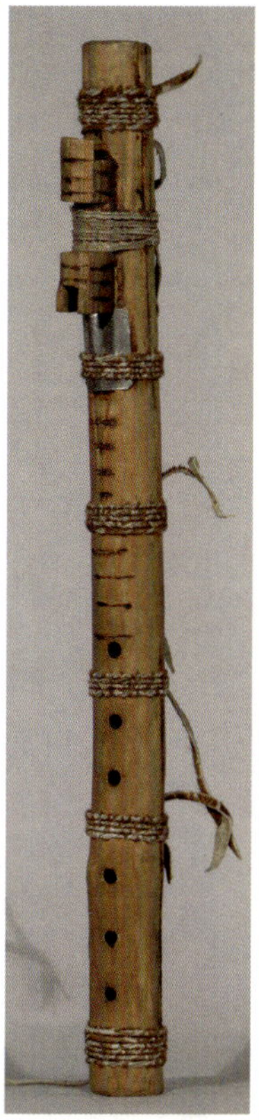

Drumming is an important part of most Indian gatherings.

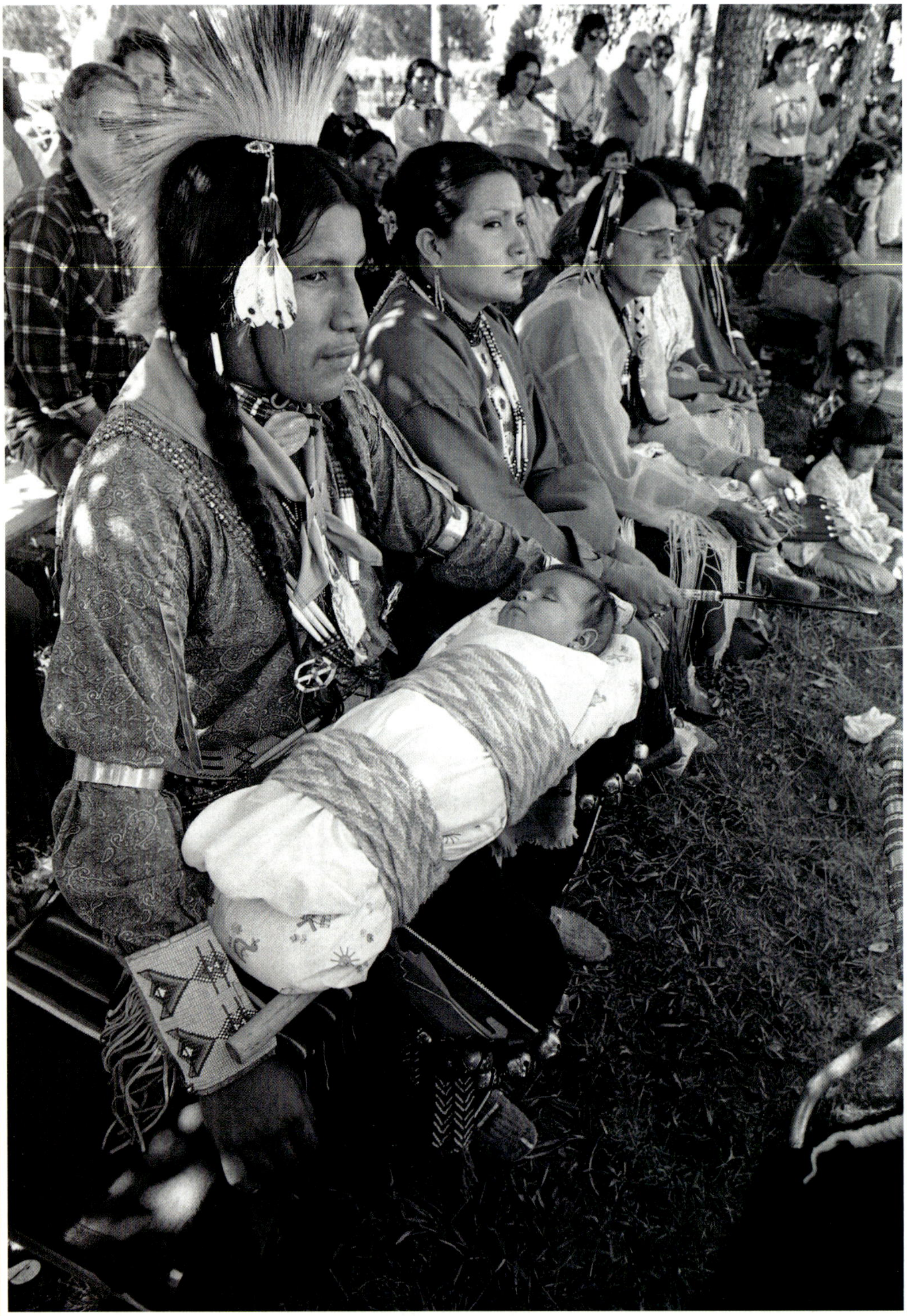

A Comanche Indian watches his infant son at a powwow in Durango, Colorado. The baby is on a cradleboard.

The Bear Dance is held in the springtime because that is when the bear awakens from its winter hibernation.

THE BEAR DANCE

Arapaho came together for the Sun Dance, a sacred time of prayer and sacrifice. The Utes would gather for the Bear Dance, a sacred celebration of springtime renewal for the entire tribe.

Tribal gatherings also provided an opportunity for young people to meet, court, and discuss marriage. They were also a time for storytelling. Telling stories, an art in itself, is how the people passed their history and heritage on to the next generation. Each tribe had its own unique myths and legends, songs, and dances.

The Colorado War (1863–1865) was an armed conflict between the United States and several allied tribes: the Kiowa, Comanche, Arapaho, and Cheyenne. The war took place on the eastern plains of what was then the Colorado Territory.

OH, PIONEERS!

The people who migrated from the eastern United States in the 1800s to settle the American West are often called American pioneers. The wilderness territories of the West were referred to as the Western or American Frontier.

CHAPTER 10

European Settlers Arrive

Suddenly, it seemed, the native people in Colorado had new neighbors. In the 1800s, white people from the eastern states began moving west in great numbers. As more and more settlers arrived in the territory, there was less room for the Indians.

The Indians and the new people had such different cultures that sharing the land was impossible. In the beginning, however, some of the people on both sides tried to live together peacefully. But thousands of new miners, farmers, ranchers, and townspeople pushed the native people off their hunting grounds.

The way the settlers saw it, nobody owned the land—not in the same legal sense that the European cultures were accustomed to. So they figured the land was free, and they took it. They considered the native people to be a dangerous nuisance. They wanted the

This illustration shows an Indian assault on a stagecoach in 1867.

Indians to go away and stay away. Some of the white people were more blunt. They wanted the Indians dead. Some of them shot great numbers of bison just to keep the Indians from having food.

The natives, of course, fought back. The way they saw it, they belonged to the land. All their ancestors belonged to the land. To them, the land was **sacred**.

What followed were several decades of dreadful bloodshed. Brutal conflicts, massacres, and wars terrorized both the native people and the new people alike.

WESTWARD HO!

Colorado men are we,
From the peaks gigantic,
from the great sierras
and the high plateaus,
From the mine and
from the gully, from the
hunting trail we come,
Pioneers! O pioneers!

—a stanza from the poem, "Pioneers! O Pioneers!" (1865) by the American poet Walt Whitman. The much longer poem is a tribute to the courage of the American pioneers.

WRANGLE UP SOME FACTS

In 1867, the U.S. Congress established the Indian Peace Commission to "remove, if possible, the causes of war." Both the Indians and the Americans wanted peace. If you were the head of this commission, what would you suggest?

CHAPTER 11

Peace Talks and Treaties

Throughout the 1800s, the U.S. government and the Indian tribes held many **peace talks**. Each time, the two sides tried to agree on the lands and the rights of the native people. Once they agreed, the parties signed a written document called a **treaty**. A treaty was a promise. Typically, the Indians would give up their claims to certain land. In return, the U.S. government might promise to provide them with food, clothing, equipment, or shelter.

In this illustration from 1835, Native Americans pass a peace pipe to a white officer at their camp, while troops wait in the distance.

The Treaty of Medicine Lodge in 1867 moved the Cheyenne and

Arapaho out of eastern Colorado. The people were sent to **reservations** in Kansas and Oklahoma. These were Indian lands that had been approved by the government. In western Colorado, the Northern Ute people were sent to a reservation in Utah in 1880. That treaty also created a reservation in the southwest corner of Colorado for the Southern Ute tribe.

For the Indians, dealings with the U.S. government were sad occasions. But treaties were worth signing if the native people would finally be left in peace and their land holdings respected. In truth, the Indians had no choice.

Chief Ignacio and Chief Ouray and their wives pose for a portrait with U.S. officials after peace talks.

"You said that you wanted to put us upon reservation, to build our houses and make us medicine lodges. I do not want them. I was born on the prairie where the wind blew free and there was nothing to break the light of the sun. ...
I know every stream and every wood between the Rio Grande and the Arkansas. I have hunted and lived over the country. I lived like my fathers before me, and like them, I lived happily."

—Comanche Chief Parry-wah-say-men (Ten Bears), at the signing of the Medicine Lodge Treaty in 1867

CHAPTER 12

How Not to Be an Indian

What if you and everyone else in your town or city were forced to move somewhere else? Not only that, you couldn't choose where to go. The government was sending you to live in this far-off place called a reservation. In the late 1800s, thousands of Indians were sent to live on reservations.

It wasn't simply a matter of moving somewhere new. The people had to give up

This is a view of the Southern Ute Agency Boarding School in Colorado in 1915.

Christian missionaries often started schools on reservations. In some cases, the U.S. government paid religious groups to provide education for Native American children.

The Ute Mountain and Southern Ute reservations in southwest Colorado are the only reservations in the state.

their entire way of life. Adapting to reservation life was difficult for the Indians. Learning new survival skills takes time. The United States wanted to quickly "Americanize" the Indians. They figured they were helping the Indians adapt to modern life—a "superior" way of life.

"NO MORE INDIANS!"

"Let us forget once and forever the word "Indian" and all that it has signified in the past, and remember only that we are dealing with so many children of a common Father."

—Charles C. Painter, a white minister, at a "Friends of the Indian" conference in 1889.

NEW NAMES

At American Indian boarding schools, children's original names were often replaced with English names. Boys were given short haircuts, which were a source of shame for boys of many tribes.

A teacher uses picture cards to instruct Navajo students in the English language in 1954.

White people at the time thought this approach was the only way Indian children might have a productive future. The white Americans also thought they were saving the Indians' souls by rescuing them from their "heathen" ways and teaching them to be Christians.

KNOWLEDGE NUGGET

SAD SCHOOLS

Conditions at Indian boarding schools were usually grim. A 1928 government report on these schools found widespread disease, poor nutrition, overcrowding, a lack of cleanliness, and children weakened by overwork.

Many native children were taken from their parents and sent to special Indian boarding schools back East where they had to speak English. Speaking their native language was forbidden. The children were taught white American culture and values. Essentially they were taught how *not* to be Indians.

Meanwhile, the adults could no longer live according to their ancestors' ways. They had to stay put and try to farm the new land, which was rarely of good quality. In other words, the people were expected to *stop* being Indians.

The Carlisle Indian Industrial School in Pennsylvania taught Indian children from many western tribes from 1879 to 1918.

DO THE RIGHT THING

"A great general has said that the only good Indian is a dead one. In a sense, I agree with the sentiment, but only in this: that all the Indian there is in the race should be dead. Kill the Indian in him and save the man."

—Richard Henry Pratt, founder of the Carlisle Indian Industrial School, in a speech in 1892. Pratt and many others like him honestly thought they were doing the right thing for the Indians.

CHAPTER 13

Colorado Indians Today

There are 566 American Indian tribes in the United States today and 325 reservations. Only two are based in Colorado—the Southern Ute tribe and the Ute Mountain tribe. Their reservations are located in the southwestern part of the state. They border on—or extend into—New Mexico.

About 80,000 Coloradans identify themselves as American Indians. Today, of course, Indians are free to live wherever they wish. Several thousand Ute people live on one of the two reservations in the state. They live and dress like any other Americans in the 21st century. They own or rent homes, drive cars, attend school, and have a wide variety of jobs. Some have gone to college and are doing very well. For many, however, life is not

WRANGLE UP SOME FACTS

American Indians were not granted U.S. citizenship until 1924.

No matter what tribe or Indian nation they belong to, Native Americans are also American citizens.

A modern-day Ute chief poses in formal tribal dress.

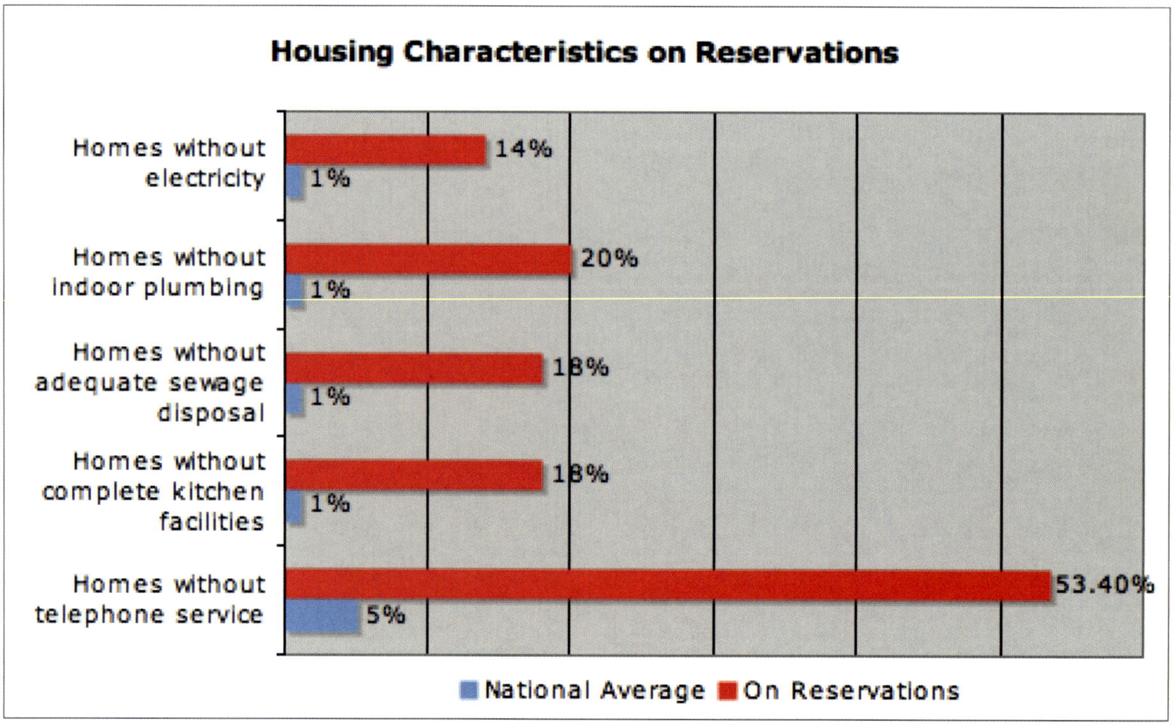

This chart compares living conditions on Indian reservations in 2011 with those of Americans in general. The percentages of homes lacking modern conveniences are much higher on reservations.

easy. More than a century after their ancestors lost their lands and way of living, many Native Americans live in poverty. A large number have health problems.

On or off the reservation, Native Americans treasure their heritage. The tribes work to keep the old customs alive. They welcome the public to their lands, to learn about the native peoples' rich culture and history.

In the spring, the Southern Utes celebrate the colorful Bear Dance. In the summer, they hold the Sun Dance, the most important spiritual ceremony in the Ute community. And in the late summer, it's time for the Southern Ute Fair Powwow.

POWWOW

KNOWLEDGE NUGGET

WHO ARE WE?

"American Indians" and "Native Americans" are both considered correct terms. In Canada, they use the term "First Nations." All these names refer to the same people. But most Native Americans prefer to identify themselves by their tribe.

Glossary

archaeologist—a scientist who studies human history by digging up human remains and artifacts

artifacts—objects made by past humans that gives clues to how they lived their lives

glacier—a slowly moving mass of ice formed by great amounts of hardened snow on mountains or near Earth's poles

ice age—a long-term period of colder temperatures on Earth, during which glaciers form on mountains and deep ice sheets cover vast areas of land. The most recent ice age is thought to have ended 10,000 years ago.

nomadic—relating to people or animals that move around from place to place, usually in tribes or groups

peace talk—a discussion about ending the hostilities, or wars, between people or groups

sacred—connected with, or dedicated to, a god or gods; holy; worthy of awe and respect

reservation—a tract of land set aside for a special purpose; an Indian reservation is an area of land managed by a Native American tribe and overseen by the US Bureau of Indian Affairs

teepee (also spelled tepee or tipi)—a cone-shaped tent made of animal skins, cloth, or canvas on a frame of poles, used by the Plains Indians

treaty—a formal written agreement between two or more nations

tribe—a social group made up of numerous families with similar values or interests

wickiup (also spelled wikiup)—an American Indian hut consisting of an oval frame covered with brushwood or grass

Index

Due to the changing nature of Internet links, the Rosen Publishing Group, Inc., has developed an online list of websites related to the subject of this book. This site is updated regularly. Please use this link to access the list: www.powerkidslinks.com/soco/tfc